Breaking the Family Curse

Testimony Still Loading...

DeAngelo Collier

Breaking the Family Curse

RiverHouse Publishing, LLC
1509 Madison Avenue
Memphis, TN 38104

Copyright © 2016 by DeAngelo Collier

All rights reserved. No part of this book may be reproduced, stored in a retrieval system or transmitted in any form or by any means without written permission of the Publisher, excepting brief quotes used in reviews.

All **RiverHouse, LLC** Titles, Imprints and Distributed Lines are available at special quantity discounts for bulk purchases for sales promotions, premiums, fund-raising and educational or institutional use.

First RiverHouse, LLC Trade Paperback Printing 05-15-2016

ISBN:

Acknowledgments

First, I would like to thank God for giving me the vision and strength to finish this powerful book. I am nothing without God. To God be the Glory. Next, I would like to thank my mother, Janice Collier for always being there for me. I also would like to acknowledge my two brothers, Rangelo Collier and Tyrone Terry, and my two sisters, Ebony Collier and Lavandalous Christion for always looking out for me. I would like to thank all of my nieces and one nephew for being in my life. I have to give thanks to my two close friends, Eric Dupree and Jasmine Aldridge for pushing and motivating me to finish this book when I wanted to give up. I wish to thank my whole family, Reginald Watkins, Artez Harris, Keshia Charleston, all of my friends, Michael Kreeger, Gilian Dean, Dr. Rodney Thomas, Mario Bradley, Megan Pietrowski, my whole Shelby County District Attorney General Office family, my hometown Gallaway, Cedar Ridge, and whoever else helped me get to where I am today. Thanks to Pastor Stephen Brown and my whole "Logic" family. Thanks to Sedrick Askew for taking my photo for the book cover, and thanks to Roderickus Pickens for designing the book cover. I would like to thank Ken Taylor for helping me set up connections to make this book a success. Last, but not least, I would like to thank the enemy for bringing adversaries after adversaries; without trials and tribulations I wouldn't be able to write this book.

Vision

I would have never imagined in a million years that I would be an author. I will never forget the night that God gave me the vision to write this book. One night, I was praying and asking God to fill me up with his love. After I was done praying, I turned on some music, and I started to reminisce about how far God has brought me. I started thinking about the goodness of God. My God! My God! Tears started to roll down my face because God had been so good to me despite my past. Despite all of the wrongs I've done, God still saw the best in me. While the tears rolled down my face, I heard God's voice speaking to me. He told me to write a book. I replied, "What did you say God?" "Are you sure you're talking to me?"

God said, "Yes I'm going to give you the strength to write the book." I was kind of afraid to take on this task at first because of my grammatical flaws, but I realized that God will never assign a task to my life designed to make me fail. I put on the armor of God, and told myself I will write this book to give God the praise. I will write this book to show people how God can turn your mess into a message. I told myself *I will write this book to help other people break their family generation curses*. I said to myself, *I will write this book to help the youth and people all around the world to not give up*. God gave me a task to complete, which is going to change lives for generations to come. I also hope this book will help someone else get out of their comfort zone and let God use them.

Table of Contents

Chapter 1 – 1
Hidden Struggle 1
Chapter 2 – 8
Family Curses 8
Chapter 3 – 10
Financial Curse 10
Chapter 4 – 13
Jail Curse 13
Chapter 5 – 17
Death Curse 17
Chapter 6 – 21
Drug Use Curse 21
Chapter 7 – 22
Education Curse 22
Chapter 8 – 24
Love Relationships Curse 24
Chapter 9 – 26
Gambling Curse 26
Chapter 10 – 28

Where Did I Go Wrong?...28

Chapter 11 –...30

Product of My Environment 30

Chapter 12 –...35

7 or 11 35

Chapter 13 –...39

Thug Life 39

Chapter 14 –...44

Fed Up 44

Chapter 15 –...46

God Found Me 46

Chapter 16 –...48

Breaking the Family Curses..48

Chapter 17 –...50

Education Soars 50

Chapter 18 –...54

Out of the Thug Life..54

Chapter 19 –...56

Spiritual Life 56

Chapter 20 –...58

Government Ties...58

Chapter 21 –...60

Giving Back 60

Chapter 22 - 62

No Drugs 62

Chapter 23 - 63

No Gambling 63

Chapter 24 - 65

Speaking Engagement 65

Chapter 25 – 67

Testimony Still Loading 67

Chapter 1 –
Hidden Struggle

I was born in Gallaway, Tennessee, which is a small town about 30 minutes outside of Memphis, Tennessee. My mother's name is Janice Collier, and my father's name is Tom Terry. I was raised in a single parent household. My mother raised me on her own. I have two brothers and two sisters. I have one brother and one sister on my mom's side and the same on my dad's side. My mother raised each of her three kids on her own. She received some help from my big sister Ebony's father, but the majority of everything my siblings and I got, which consisted of love, clothes, food, and shelter came from my mother. If I had a thousand tongues, I still wouldn't be able to tell my mom how much I love her and appreciate all of the sacrifices she made to take care of my siblings and me.

I lived in Gallaway up to the age of six before moving to Memphis. I grew up in the Raleigh area of Memphis. I didn't grow up with a silver spoon, but my mother kind of made it seem as if I did.

All the way up to the age of thirteen I never had a bad Christmas. I never realized all of the enjoyment that I got from getting everything I wanted for Christmas really came from my mother working her butt off and stressing. The gifts came from restless nights of my mother thinking about how she was going to make sure that my siblings and I had the best Christmas ever every year. If I would've been aware and had a conscious mindset as a child that the enjoyment in everything I got for Christmas came from sleepless nights, headaches, and my mom asking God how was she going to make our Christmas good, I would've told my mother "never mind I can go without." As I got older, I started to become more attentive to my mother's financial struggle and realized that my mother worked her butt off and did whatever she had to do to make sure I had everything I wanted. My mom had several jobs in her life but none of the jobs was a career job.

My mom received a lot of help from the government. She was and still is on Section 8, a government assistance housing program for low income families. She also used to receive EBT food stamps. EBT food stamps are monthly food vouchers that the government gives to low income families. Unfortunately, the food stamps that we use to receive on a monthly basics weren't always enough to feed us for the whole month, but I am thankful for the few food stamps that we did get. I remember countless days when my mother had to scuffle or borrow money from people in order for us to satisfy our hunger. One thing I can say, God always made a way for my mother to feed us.

Another struggle I became familiar with was not having transportation to get around. My mother had a car all the way up until I was nine or ten years old. I will never forget the time my mother leased a 2002 Ford Explorer. She bought the Ford Explorer with her tax refund money. A couple of months went by and she had gotten behind on her car note. She had to hide the truck from the repo man until one day she got tired of dodging him. The repo man came and took our only source of transportation away. Without our car it was difficult for us to get around. My siblings and I attended schools in Frayser at the time, which were about five miles from our house. Our schools were only ten minutes driving distance, but imagine us walking every day back and forth to school. No way. My siblings and I could not have done that every day. My mother had to come up with a plan, because we couldn't miss school. We needed our education. The only reliable transportation we could think of was the Mata bus. We hated riding the bus, but we had to do what we had to do. We had to wake up around 5:30 am. every morning to catch the bus to my auntie Vonnie's house. Once we got off at the bus stop we had to walk about a mile to my auntie's house because school didn't start until 7:00 am. Not only that, my cousins and I had to walk another mile from my auntie's house to school. The school didn't have bus routes that stopped by my auntie's house. My siblings and I used to be so exhausted from walking when we got home from school, but we made it work.

My mom always dressed me in decent clothes when I went to school until times started to get difficult. I remember one year in middle school, right before school started my mother didn't have any money to buy me some new school clothes. Everybody knows that all kids like to wear new clothes and shoes to start the school year off right. I was fourteen years old at the time. I was so afraid to go to school on the first day without new clothes and shoes. My mom didn't have any money to buy me some. Nevertheless, God made a way for us. My mom won some money at the casino to buy me some new school clothes. I was so happy, but little did I know I was about to face the same problem in middle school.

I will never forget about the time in middle school when I didn't have a lot of school clothes and shoes. I was in the eighth grade. I only had three pairs of uniform pants — khaki, blue, and black. The black pair was too short, and I had to put rubber bands on the legs so my classmates wouldn't talk about me. The rubber bands made it seem like my pants weren't too short. The khakis and black uniform pants fit perfectly. I had to make those three pairs of uniform pants last me until the end of the school year. I wore the khakis on Mondays and Fridays. I wore the blue pants on Tuesdays and Thursdays, and I wore the black ones on Wednesdays. Also, I only had two white uniform shirts that lasted me the whole school year. We didn't have a washer at the time, and sometimes I had to wear my uniform more than once without washing it.

I only had one pair of shoes. I had a pair of Nike white air force ones that my mom had bought me. I wore the white air force ones so much that they were no longer white; they were cream. I will never forget the too little black air force ones that I had to ask my sister to wear because I was tired of wearing the white air force ones. I wore a size seven at the time and my sister's shoes were a size six. I had to take the soles out of the shoes, but the shoes were still too little. The struggle was real, but I was still blessed.

I made a promise to myself before I started writing this book that I would write about every struggle that I've been through that I could remember. In middle school, my favorite thing to do when I got home from school was watch PBS kids while I ate a fried double bologna sandwich with cheese. I watched Dragon Tales every day of the week, and if I missed it I would get highly upset.

Dragon Tales was my favorite cartoon show. I remember having cable a few times but it wasn't consistent. For amusement on Saturdays, I would wake up early in the morning to catch the cartoon shows on basic television or go outside and jump on the trampoline that my mom bought me. I don't know how but my brother and I always had the latest game systems and games. I guess my mom's winnings from card games and the casino were serving her well.

My mom was a heavy gambler. She used to gamble playing card games and at the casino. Deuce of Wild is a card game that people bet money on against each other. My mom used to win a lot in those card games, but she also lost a lot of money. My mother used to spend countless nights at the casino so she could have all of her bill money and provide for her kids. I can say my mother has been to every casino in Tunica, Mississippi, but I love my mother for making a way out of no way.

A few times she pawned some of my siblings' and my amusement toys to pay the bills. I always got sad when she did that but my siblings knew that our lights would be cut off if she didn't. I didn't understand at the time, because I liked my toys and stuff. I remembered one time my mom had bought me a brand new PlayStation Portable game. Unfortunately, my mom had to pawn my game so she could pay a bill.

Through all the good and bad days, my mother taught me the true definition of embracing the struggle. She taught me to never look like what I was going through. My mother always made a way for her children no matter what, even if she had to do it on her own. I had everything I needed when I was a child. I never had a bad Christmas or a bad birthday. But when I got older, everything changed. The struggle got real. I have to become successful because my mom had to sacrifice a lot of things so my siblings and I could have a good life. I promise I will be successful, and nothing will stop me. I have to show my mother that I did not take for granted all of her hard work, struggling, and stress.

Chapter 2 – Family Curses

My family "The Colliers" has been around for a long time. My family is originally from Olive Branch, Mississippi. My grandfather, Ephraim Collier, who passed away the same year I was born, met my grandmother in Olive Branch. My grandfather moved his family to Gallaway, Tennessee when his job was relocated. My grandmother, Vernett Collier, told me that she was scared to move because the town of Gallaway was in another state. She didn't know anybody there. My grandparents raised their family in Gallaway. I have four aunties and two uncles on my mom's side of the family. I have about fifty first cousins on my mom's side. My family is pretty big. I never knew anybody on my father's side of the family until the year 2014; that's when I met my older brother and sister on my dad's side. I really don't know a lot of my family members on my father's side except my sister Lavandalous and my brother Tyrone.

My family has not been living up to its full potential. The devil has been riding my family for a very long time, and I'm sick of it. The devil will no longer get the satisfaction from having a chain around my family's neck. My family has a lot of potential and we will rise up against the enemy's plans. The devil has been attacking my family financially, mentally, and spiritually.

Chapter 3 – Financial Curse

One of the areas the devil has been fighting my family in is our financial status. I understand that money doesn't always produce happiness, but I want my family to have the finer things in life. I want my family to be able to just wake up and take vacations on a regular basis. I want my family to not have to stress over bills. Everything that I say about my family is not intended to degrade us, but to shed light on my family's generational curses. I want the world to know about the obstacles and curses that my family had to endure before the overflow of blessings come.

My family is not a wealthy family. No one in my family has made more than 40k a year in legal money yet. There are no business owners in my family yet. The majority of the members of my family currently work for warehouses and have worked for warehouses for some years including me. One of my aunties and one of my uncles never had a job a day of their life. How can a person possibly survive without a job? My auntie has been on government assistance for as long as I can remember, and my uncle has been a hustler for as long as I can remember. My auntie has high blood pressure and that forbids her from getting a job; this reduces her chances of making money. As I stated earlier, government assistance is offered to people who have financial problems, and those who have disabilities.

Government assistance consists of housing assistance, EBT food stamps, health insurance, and more. My family including myself has been on housing assistance, EBT food stamps, and government health insurance for a long time. More than half of my aunties including my mama have gotten food stamps or been on Section 8 all of their life, and that kind of *grinds my gears*. I know what kind of potential my family has. We were created to live comfortably and financially free. Being on government assistant restricts that. When a person is on government assistance the government has the advantage of controlling you. If you get housing assistance, the government will not let you get a job. If you get a job, the government will take you off government assistant. I think some of my family members are afraid to get off government assistant because they are comfortable.

I hate that some of my family has to rely on the government just to survive, but that's all my family has known. I have to give credit to the people in my family who aren't on government assistance. I'm glad that some of my family members are stepping up to break that curse. We will step out of our comfort zone to become financially free. Some of my family members will make more than eighty thousand dollars a year in legal money. We will have business owners in the family. We will be able to go on vacations anytime that we want to. The financial chains are being broken right now. We all will be financially free!

Chapter 4 –
Jail Curse

Another curse my family has been dealing with for generations is getting into trouble with the law. This seems like one of the hardest areas in which the enemy has been attacking my family. It seems like every time one of my family members gets out of jail, another one goes in. Every man in my family except two of us has been to jail at least one time. Note that there are about fifteen men in my family over the age of eighteen. I've been to jail once in my life. I have a cousin who is almost the same age as I am who went to jail in November 2015. My cousin is locked up for selling drugs and for money laundering. He is only twenty-two years of age. He has three little beautiful girls whom he probably won't see for a long time.

My cousin always had problems with the law. My cousin had a secret indictment charge on him when he was only fifteen years old. Fifteen years old is very young to be having the police watching you. My cousin and I grew up together. We were like two peas in a pod. I hate that so much that he is in prison. My cousin was supposed to graduate from high school and make something positive out of himself, but the devil got hold of him. My cousin was a very talented football and basketball player. My cousin won a lot of football trophies, but he couldn't resist the streets. He got caught up in the street life and never looked back. The enemy was letting the money look too good to my cousin such that he got sidetracked and fell off course. I wish he was more aware of the enemy attacks because 1 Peter 5:8 declares, "Be sober, be vigilant; because your adversary the devil, as a roaring lion, walketh about, seeking whom he may devour (KJV)."

My cousin is locked up for trying to provide for his family. I know selling drugs isn't the right way to feed your family, but what do you expect him to do when hustling in an illegal way was the only thing he saw growing up? His daddy wasn't a great role model. His daddy always was in jail. What do you expect from a teenager who is not rooted in God to do when his or her back is against the wall? My auntie, his mom, was already struggling, and he felt like he had to get out into the streets to provide for her. What do you expect from a teenager who doesn't have any positive role models or mentors? What do you expect when the streets are constantly knocking at the door?

Exactly! It seems as if my family has been answering the door for the streets. This puts a burden on my family, but that curse is being broken right now. I promise my cousin is going to turn his life around when he get out of jail. God will make a way for him to get back on the right track, and I am stepping up to become a positive role model for my family. None of my family members who are younger than I am will be in the jail system. My family members who are older than I am will not step another foot in jail. The government will no longer see my family unless it is for doing something positive.

I have learned from the pain and sorrow that some of my family members have put my family through from being incarcerated. Being in jail puts a burden on every person who loves you. People might not think about the effects that their decisions are going to have on their loved ones during the time of the act, but it will definitely hurt them. Being incarcerated hurts your family mentality, financially, and socially.

I remember one of my cousins was sentenced to five years in prison, and I can't count on my two hands how many times my auntie cried because her son was locked up. My auntie stressed the whole five years her oldest son was in prison. My auntie did all she could to keep money on my cousin's commissary and that caused some of her other children to miss out on some things. My auntie's children missed out on several Christmases because my auntie was trying to help my incarcerated cousin out. Christmas is one of the most important times of the year for teenagers and kids. Not receiving anything for Christmas as a child felt like your whole life was crushed. Not only did my cousin have a mother who was struggling financially and physically, but he also missed out on a lot of family time.

Nothing good comes from being incarcerated. When you're in jail your love ones have to continually put money on your commissary. What if your family is already struggling to keep the bills paid? How will you get commissary? Being incarcerated also hurts your loved ones socially. You won't be able to attend any family gatherings. The only way you can talk to your loved ones is over the phone, and the only way you can see them is through a window. You're only allowed to have visitors on certain days. Let's face it, jail is definitely not a place where anybody wants to be. This curse is being broken in my family life. None of my family will become victims of the jail cell. We all will be free!

Chapter 5 – Death Curse

Death has been one of the most continual curses that my family has had to deal with for the past eight years. The first death in my family to occur was that of my grandfather, Ephraim. My grandfather died the same year I was born, and I didn't get a chance to bond with him. I hate that so much. Death didn't hit my family again until the year 2007.

The death of my older cousin Kendrick Collier hit my family unexpectedly. I will never forget the night my cousin Kendrick got stabbed to death. I was lying in bed while my brother and cousins were playing card games. My cousin Kerterter called my mother and said, "Kendrick just got stabbed." We arrived there and found out Kendrick had been stabbed in the heart. Kendrick died on the scene. The craziest thing about my cousin's death is that the dude that killed my cousin was very close to him. The killer's family and my family were very close. My cousin and his killer treated each other like best friends, well at least that is what we thought. I questioned God so many times about my cousin's death. I asked God how my cousin died from a stab wound when in the past he got shot fifteen times, eight on one occasion and seven on the other and still survived. Kendrick's death hit my family hard and we're still dealing with it.

Unfortunately, Kendrick's death was the first of many. Within an eight year span five people very close to me passed away. I never knew death would be so hard to cope with. The next death that occurred was that of my favorite cousin, Taveo Collier in 2010. Taveo died from a four-wheeler accident. His death caught me totally by surprise. I never thought somebody that close to me would just slip away like that. I still remember the day he died. I was in summer school trying to graduate a year early than I was supposed to. I was on my phone in class, and I saw a post from my cousin Brittany that read "pray for Taveo." I instantly called her to ask her what happened. She replied, "Taveo has just been in a four-wheeler accident." My heart dropped when she told me that. I almost got kicked out of summer school that day because I was trying to leave early. I miss my favorite cousin, Taveo. We always used to be around each other. He treated me like his little brother. I'm still mourning his death, but I know God makes no mistakes. Deaths after deaths occur, but I know God will see my family through.

Most of my loved ones who died got taken away from me in the hands of another person. Four out of the five of my loved ones got killed by somebody, and that's extremely sad.

My second loved one who got killed was named Marquez. Marquez's death caught me by surprise, because Taveo had died two weeks prior to him. Marquez had texted me the same day Taveo died and asked if I was alright. Two weeks later I received a text message in summer school that read "Marquez has just been shot." I never lost two people that were very close to me in one month until that year. My pain was running deeper than the ocean. It felt like my whole life was falling apart. I was holding in so much pain; I never showed my pain on the outside. The only thing I was holding to was faith. How could I possibly lose two of my loved ones two weeks apart?

After those two deaths, I thought it couldn't get any worse, but I was wrong. One of the hardest deaths to ever hit my life was the death of my play brother Michael. Michael got killed on March 12th, 2014. I still remember when I got that phone call from my friend ShayShay. She called me hollering saying, "Lil Mike had just got shot." I told her to stop lying because I couldn't believe it. I instantly went over to his mom's house, and she told me it was true. Michael's death was one of the worst deaths I ever had to deal with. I'm getting teary eyed while I write this. I treated Michael like a little brother. He had faith in me, and he made me believe. I still can't believe that my little brother is gone. He died right before spring break 2014, and I really wasn't in the mood to go anywhere. My whole mood changed, but I went anyway. I will never forget about him. He will forever live through me. I know that Michael is in a better place.

The last death that hit my family was the death of my cousin-in-law, Darius. Darius just got out of jail two weeks before his death. His death was a horrible tragedy. Darius died from a gunshot wound. My two little cousins have to grow up without their real father. I'm sick of losing my family to stuff that could've easily been avoided. All of my loved ones are supposed to be living right now, but we can't control death. My family will become better. My family will live long lives. This curse is being broken right now! Rest in peace to all of my loved ones.

Chapter 6 –
Drug Use Curse

One curse I want my family to break is that of doing drugs. This is not a big curse in my family but it is noticeable. Most of my older cousins smoke marijuana. Also, I have people in my family who pop pills, and do powder cocaine too. It's only a selected few who pop pills and do powder cocaine. I'm so ready for this curse to break in my family. Smoking marijuana is not good. Taking pills for your personal use can mess your body up, and I definitely don't want any of my family members' health to be in jeopardy from taking illegal pills. The same goes for doing powder cocaine. I thank God nobody in my family has overdosed on drugs. I am very thankful for that, but the doing drugs stronghold on my family will be broken in the name of Jesus.

Chapter 7 – Education Curse

Everybody knows that education is one of the most important things a person can attain to make it in this world. Education is very vital, but education has had a negative stronghold on my family. As far as education goes, my family does not hold a lot of diplomas and degrees. My family is not educated, but they aren't slow either. Only about ten people out of my whole family have a high school diploma. Most of all my aunties and uncles dropped out in middle school. One of my uncles dropped out of school in the sixth grade, and one of my aunties dropped out of school in the eighth grade. I don't know what was going through their heads at the time, but I wish they would've gotten their high school diploma. I wish they would've graduated from college. Out of all my grandmother's kids, only one of them completed high school. Note this, my grandmother has seven kids. Only about half of my grandmother's grandkids eighteen or over have graduated from high school.

My favorite boy cousin who I mentioned earlier with the secret indictment dropped out of high school in the ninth grade. I hate that so bad for my cousin. He had the potential to get his high school diploma, but he will go back to get his GED. Only three people out of my whole family graduated from college. Nobody in my family has graduated from college with a Bachelors' degree, but that's going to change. I know that God is turning around the educational curse in my family, because I will graduate in 2016 with my BA. The educational curse will be broken, and I'm saying that with confidence. I stand on God's word that the yoke is being broken from over my family.

Chapter 8 –
Love Relationships Curse

Love relationships in my family are not so great. I have only been to two weddings in my whole life and neither one of them consisted of my family members. Only three people in my family have been married. Two of my aunties are married and one of my cousins is married. It seems like everybody in my family has had a baby out of wedlock. I was born out of wedlock.

Most of the women in my family have been in hurtful relationships. Most of all their ex-boyfriends have not had strong relationships with God. Most of them were gangbangers, weed smokers, and drug sellers. I'm not downing any of them because I love all of them. I treated them all like family, but I have to shed light on this curse in my family life. I have to shed light because this curse can't continue to hold the women in my family down.

The men's love relationships in my family aren't that good neither. Most of them cheat on their spouses, and have babies out of wedlock. Some of them don't take care of their children, but that's about to change. God is turning this curse around. Moving forward, none of my family members will have babies out of wedlock. None of my family members will be used as sex slaves. The men in my family will treat their women like queens. They will no longer cheat on their spouses. All of them will be the providers in the relationship. Everybody's relationships in my family will be driven by Christ!

Chapter 9 – Gambling Curse

Gambling has been an ongoing generational curse in my family. For as long as I can remember, my family has been addicted to gambling. My family gambles against each other, and against non-family members. Every time we have a family gathering, gambling always has to occur. Gambling amongst each other has led to fallouts, and fights. I remember one time, two of my cousins got into a big fight with each other. One of them had cheated in the dice game, and the other one got mad.

My family plays card games, goes to the casino, and shoots dice. At every family gathering somebody has to bring out the cards. We always try to find ways to make money, and gambling is a quick way to do that. Nevertheless, a person would think that playing cards is the biggest gambling addiction that my family has but that is not true. I must say gambling at the casino has to be my family's biggest gambling addiction. Everybody twenty-one or over in my family has been to the casino at least one time in their life. I've been to the casino four times, and I regretted every time that I went. Every time I think about going to the casino, something inside of me stops me from going. I take a moment to think about how the generation gambling curse has affected my family.

My mother told me that my grandmother used to be addicted to the casino, and she followed in her footsteps. My mother, brother, and a couple of my cousins go to the casino at least one time a week. Everybody in my family started off gambling around age fourteen. We learned how to play cards watching the generation ahead of us. My mother's generation learned how to gamble from my grandmother's generation. My brother's generation learned how to gamble from my mother's generation. My generation learned how to play from my brother's generation, but the gambling curse is stopping with my generation. My family will no longer take part in gambling.

The devil will not continue to have a curse over my family life. The yoke is being broken. Financial problems, jail problems, death, relationship problems, drug problems, and gambling problems will no longer be an issue in my family. God is restoring everything that the devil has taken from my family. The Collier family will be everything that God intended us to be.

Chapter 10 – Where Did I Go Wrong?

Before I go into details about how I have broken some of my family curses, I have to first address the issues I was dealing with. I have to let the world know about some of the mistakes I made as a teenager. I have to tell the world about the kind of life I was living before I realized my purpose in life. Everything I did didn't come from my mom's parenting. My mother raised me to be a respectful young man. All of the bad decisions I made weren't because of the way my mother raised me. My mother did all she could raising me by herself, and I love her for that. She did a great job. Don't get the wrong perception that my mother spared the rod on me, because she wasn't aware of all the wrong that I was doing. I knew my mom would beat my tail if I would've told her about the gambling, fighting, and the neighborhood foolishness.

In my teenage years, I was well behaved until I got to high school, well until I got to Cedar Ridge. When I attended Raleigh Egypt Middle School I made all A's and hung around people who were making the same grades as I was. Raleigh Egypt had a bad reputation, but I was in an honors class and took part in a science club. I behaved pretty well in middle school. I never received an out-of-school suspension or an in-school suspension. I don't even think the principals knew me by my name. That is how well behaved I was in middle school. I was known in school as the quiet dude. But all of that changed when my favorite auntie, Vonnie moved to a subdivision in Memphis called Cedar Ridge.

Cedar Ridge is a neighborhood in Raleigh. My auntie moved to that neighborhood after my cousin Kendrick got killed. My auntie moved to Cedar Ridge in the summer of 2008. I started going over to my auntie's house a lot, because I was bored at my house. During that time, I became friends with a lot of people in the neighborhood. I became so close with the teenagers in Cedar Ridge that I persuaded my mom to let me attend high school with them. I didn't want to attend Raleigh Egypt High School, which was the school assigned to my mom's address. I didn't used to hang around a lot of people who attended Raleigh Egypt. Everybody who I hung around at the time was attending Bolton, and that's how all the chaos started.

Chapter 11 –
Product of My Environment

I never understood the saying "you're a product of your environment" until I started to hang out in Cedar Ridge. I never knew how much power and influence my surroundings had over my life. I was so caught up in trying to do what the cool kids were doing that I lost sight of myself. I lost sight of all the hard work my mom did raising me by herself to become a wise young man. The environment in Cedar Ridge was so appealing to my mind at the time that it almost messed up my whole life.

Cedar Ridge was a neighborhood full of young and middle aged people. There were so many teenagers in the neighborhood at the time that we came up with a name to represent ourselves. We changed the name from Cedar Ridge to "CRG." CRG is an acronym for Cedar Ridge Goons. We thought that "Cedar Ridge Goons" defined us. We were young and reckless.

The living conditions in Cedar Ridge were decent even though some of the houses were on Section 8. A random person riding through the neighborhood wouldn't have considered Cedar

Ridge to be the ghetto, but if that person would've gotten out the car and roamed around the neighborhood for a few hours I bet that person's outlook would've changed. That person would've come in contact with gamblers, gang members, illegal gun carriers, etc.

Cedar Ridge was like a big family. We treated each other like brothers, sisters, and cousins. The majority of people got along with each other. Of course we had altercations with each other, but that's what families do. After we fought each other we got back "cool" within the next week, but when we fought an outsider we never got back "cool." Every time a person in Cedar Ridge got into an argument with an outsider, the whole neighborhood would be ready to fight that person. The love in the neighborhood was great, and everybody looked out for each other. We stuck together in the neighborhood, at parties, and at school.

The environment in Cedar Ridge played a vital role in shaping my mind frame and everything that I indulged in during my teenage years. I was so blinded by trying to fit in with the crowd that I lost sight of myself. I was physically in my body but I was letting other people think for me. I was letting the environment in Cedar Ridge shape me. When you let other people and things shape your mind, you lose sight of what God has for your life.

I already had a gambling habit, because of my family but it got worse after I began to hang out in Cedar Ridge. I already knew how to shoot dice because of my family, but because of hanging around in Cedar Ridge it became an everyday thing.

When I took a look on everything I did in Cedar Ridge, I realized I made some crazy mistakes. I was influenced in so many different ways by the surroundings in Cedar Ridge. Most of the people I hung around were gamblers, gangbangers, lusters, fighters, and robbers. When I got to Cedar Ridge I became friends with the whole neighborhood and that's what started it all. I was vulnerable because I was used to being in the house all day, every day. Please don't get me wrong. I still had love for everybody in Cedar Ridge. They didn't pressure me to do anything. I take full responsibility for my actions. Unfortunately, I don't think I would've indulged in certain things if I wasn't in Cedar Ridge. Also, I'm not trying to degrade Cedar Ridge or the people whom I hung around in Cedar Ridge. I know I influenced teenagers in Cedar Ridge to indulge in bad things, and I apologize for my actions. Some of my actions in Cedar Ridge influenced people to lose money, to get into gangs, and to fight.

The environment, the type of people I hung around, and my actions led me to get arrested. I went to jail in 2012 for a crime I didn't commit. I almost messed my future up from hanging around the wrong crowd. Also, I was being disobedient to my mom because she sent me over to my auntie house to pick something up for her, but I ended up staying longer after I saw a couple of friends. My friends and I were hanging out behind an abandoned house and the neighbors called the police on us. When the police arrived, two of my friends ran in the opposite direction from the police and the rest walked to the front of the house because we weren't doing anything illegal. The police made my friends and me sit on the curb in front of the house. One of the police officers came back to the front of the house with some cargo pants in his hand. He reached in the cargo pockets and found a half ounce of marijuana. He asked us whose marijuana was it. We told him the truth that the illegal drugs weren't ours, but the police still took all four of us to jail. I was afraid the whole time I was in jail because my future was at stake. My whole future was in the hands of another person. I could've missed out on my dreams because of the wrong crowd I was hanging around. I would've been contributing to my family's generational curse, but the judge dismissed the case. The judge found out that I should've not gotten arrested. I thank God for giving me a second chance to do right. I thank

God for the favor. My life could've been over. I'm glad God allowed the judge to see the truth.

Hanging around the wrong crowd can get a person in trouble. Why hang around people who don't motivate you or push you to be great? Why hang around people who don't care about their own future? I had to open my eyes and realize that I was putting my freedom and my life in jeopardy by hanging around the wrong crowd. I had to change my circle. I had to surround myself with people who were trying to become successful the right way. I had to switch my circle to people who were scared of failing. I'm glad that God allowed me a second chance to get on the right path. I'm forever grateful for that. God is everything. God turned my mess into a message.

Chapter 12 –
7 or 11

Gambling was one of the biggest trials I had to face in my life thus far, but my gambling addiction didn't just come out of nowhere. My family consists of people with gambling addictions, and I had no choice but to follow in their footsteps. I first started gambling when I was about thirteen years old. I only gambled at family gatherings. As I got older, my gambling got worse. I really wasn't a heavy gambler until I started to hang out in Cedar Ridge. Gambling was one of the biggest negative influences Cedar Ridge had on my life. I already knew how to shoot dice before I got to Cedar Ridge, but I wasn't shooting dice every day until I got over there.

Shooting dice was my biggest gambling addiction. I was so addicted to shooting dice that I often lied to my mother about the money that she gave me. I remember this one time, some new Jordan shoes were coming out that following Saturday. I asked my mother if she would buy them for me and she said "yeah." My mother gave me a $100 so my friend could go to the Nike factory to buy the new shoes for me. I was over my auntie's house in Cedar Ridge at the time, and she took the money over there to me. As soon as my mother left my auntie's house, one of my friends in the neighborhood texted me about shooting dice. My friend told me this dude who was known for shooting dice was trying to gamble against us. I was so sprung off gambling and making fast money that I wasn't worried about the fact that my mother had just given me a hundred dollars of her hard earned money to buy some shoes. I instantly replied to my friend, "I'm on my way to the cove."

The cove was an area in the neighborhood that everybody chilled at. The cove was the heart of the neighborhood. Everybody knew to go to the cove for the latest action. We shot dice in the cove, fought in the cove, chilled in the cove, and played basketball in the cove. So, my mother had trusted me enough to give my friend the money for my shoes, but I had let her down. I lost all of the money that my mom gave me shooting dice, and I felt so bad. She asked me about the shoes, and I had to make up a lie to cover up my gambling addiction. It was so hard lying to my mom about the money. I had to tell a lie to my mom about something that could've easily been avoided if I would've been obedient. It all dated back to the gambling generation curse that the enemy has placed over my family life. Also, gambling on the street is a dangerous thing to do, and I most definitely had my share.

Gambling on the street opened my eyes to so many things that I thought I never would've experienced. I have seen people get robbed and get beat up right in front of me because of shooting dice. I'm talking about people who got stripped out of their clothes right in front of me. I always have been a kindhearted person, and stuff like that used to get under my skin. I remember this one particular time I was shooting dice in Cedar Ridge. It was about six of us shooting dice outside in broad daylight. We were on top on the hill in the cove. Three of the dudes were from another part of Memphis, and they came to Cedar Ridge just to shoot dice with us. Out of nowhere, one of the dudes pulled out a gun and pointed it at a dude who stayed in the neighborhood. I watched the whole robbery take place right in front of my eyes. He made the dude strip all the way down to his draws, and the robber took all of his money. I couldn't believe that was happening right in front of me. I still didn't learn my lesson from that incident. God gave me signs after signs to give up my gambling addiction, but I refused to listen.

You never know what gambling can lead to, and on several different occasions God saved me from danger. I remember this one time, a couple of associates and I were shooting dice at my auntie's house. I will never forget what happened on that day. In the middle of the dice game, my mother called me and told me she wanted me to come babysit my niece while she went to the casino. She picked me up and dropped me off at my sister's house. I can't make this up. As soon as I walked inside my sister's house, one of my friends with whom I was shooting dice at my auntie's house called me. He called and said three dudes just busted inside my auntie's house and robbed them. The three dudes pointed the gun at everybody in the house and demanded money. Thank God nobody got hurt during the robbery. At that very instance I knew I had to stop shooting dice before it ended up getting me hurt. I was doing very well for a few months until that gambling urge came back.

Shooting dice can put people in dangerous situations that sometimes can lead to death. Shooting dice can lead a person to get robbed. Why would somebody want to lose their life over money? There are plenty of ways to make money the legal way. We have to think smarter and make a living the right way!

Chapter 13 – Thug Life

Growing up I was aware of the street life, but I never associated myself with being in the streets until I got to Cedar Ridge. In middle school, I hung around the smart kids, and one can say that I was a quiet person. I never got into any trouble in middle school, and I don't even think the principals knew me. The only time I interacted with the principals was when I received an academic award. I never got into trouble in school or at home, but I knew the game of the streets. Being around my family taught me the game, but I never let that side come out of me during my early teenage years. I never got into a fight during my middle school years, and my middle school years went by smoothly without me getting into trouble. Unfortunately, I can't say the same about my high school years. I was involved in fights after fights. I got kind of rough around the edges my freshman year at Bolton High School.

Bolton High School was the school that everybody in the neighborhood attended. We had people who didn't stay in Cedar Ridge who attended Bolton just because they always hung out in the neighborhood. We were the most known neighborhood in the school. We also were known for keeping up the most trouble at school. Things had gotten so bad at Bolton that the administrators labeled Cedar Ridge a gang. We had such a bad reputation that the administrators put the whole Cedar Ridge in the gang book. I know this is kind of crazy to say but the truth be told if the youth of Cedar Ridge were assigned to another school, Bolton would've been one of the best schools in the school district.

The drama from school often led to us acting out at the bus stop. Fighting, and gambling were part of the norm activities that occurred at the afternoon bus stop. The fighting occurred so often that the police had to be at the bus stop almost every time that we arrived in the neighborhood. Every day after school a police officer had to be at our bus stop. We had fights in the neighborhood at least two times a week.

All of the principals at Bolton High School knew me by my full name and nickname. The principals knew me because I always stayed in their offices. The administrators labeled me as a product of Cedar Ridge, and I totally agreed with them. Most of the confrontations at Cedar Ridge started in the neighborhood. The principals always had the scoop on what happened in Cedar Ridge. We were known for beating people up. Thinking back on the times how we made a name for ourselves, I'm so disappointed with myself. We used to start fights at school for fun. I remember this one time one of the dudes from Cedar Ridge had beaten two dudes up for no reason at school. I was real cool with one of the dudes who got beat up, but I couldn't help him. I couldn't help him because he got beaten up by a dude from Cedar Ridge. I couldn't break the Cedar Ridge code.

Cedar Ridge had so many enemies. I remember this one time, we had problems with the neighborhood that was beside us. This one particular day, everybody was standing outside in the cove. We were chilling in the cove and out of nowhere one of my Cedar Ridge friends came running through the cut. A cut is another name for a shortcut that makes it easy for people to get somewhere quicker on foot. We had made a cut that made it easy for us to get to the other neighborhoods. So, one of my friends came running through the cut. He told us that the people in the next neighborhood tried to jump him. At that very moment, everybody stopped what they were doing and ran over to the next neighborhood. There were about twenty-five of us and all of us fought against the dudes who tried to jump our friend. I know that was a crazy and an uncivilized thing to do, but that was how we operated. If one person fought, we all fought. We all stood for the same thing, and played by the same rules.

Fighting was something Cedar Ridge was publicly known for. We had made a name for ourselves that we were not fit to be messed with. We used to beat people up for no reason at all. We always fought at parties. Cedar Ridge had a lot of enemies. I remember this one time a couple of people and I were at this party. We saw a group of our enemies at the party. I will never forget what happen as we were about to leave the party. We were standing in front of the entrance and out of nowhere we heard gunshots. Our revival's gang members were doing a drive-by shooting on us. I was so scared. As soon as I heard bullets hitting the glass and door behind us, I ran. I thought one of us had been shot because the rival gang members were shooting directly at us. I thank God that none of us got shot that night. God was definitely with us, and I'm forever grateful.

Fighting has put me in a lot of dangerous situations. I have gotten shot at on numerous occasions. When I think about all of the times I fought, I realize that I was being stupid. All of those fights were pointless and I am so thankful that I didn't end up in jail or dead as a result. We should love each other and build each other up instead of fighting each other. I'm so glad that God has changed my mindset because I don't know where I would be if he hadn't.

Chapter 14 – Fed Up

I never knew that my life would be how it is right now, and I thank God for that. I still remember the time I got fed up with all of the wrong I was doing. I was fighting, gambling, and hanging around the wrong crowd. One night I lay down and took a look at my whole life and everything that was happening around me after I got out of jail. Everything I ever dreamed about accomplishing could've been gone because of the company I kept around me. I thank God that he had his hands on me in the courtroom. My dream is to become an FBI agent and if the enemy would've had his way with me that dream would've been gone. I can't be an FBI agent with a criminal record. My whole life would've crashed. That little incident opened up my eyes for the better.

    I told myself that I had to change the environment that I was in. I knew that I had to separate myself from the things that didn't contribute to the dreams I wanted to come true. I knew I had to separate myself from people who would get me in trouble and from people who could've gotten me hurt. What if I would've been convicted for a crime that I didn't even commit? My mother and family would've been devastated. My freedom would've been taken away. Even if I would've lost my life in the streets that would've put a burden on my mama and my family. I had to change my way of thinking and separate myself from the wrong crowd. God saved my future and I'm forever thankful for that.

I also was fed up with losing my loved ones to the grave and jail cells because of the streets. I couldn't continue to let that curse terrorize my family. I lost too many loved ones from incarceration, and the graveyard from being in the streets. Some of my cousins and uncles missed their children's birthdays because they were locked up. I will never again see any of my cousins who are dead. I hate that so much. They left behind so many people who loved them, and because of that I had to change my life around. I couldn't continue be a product of my environment!

Chapter 15 – God Found Me

God has been so merciful to me and I will forever give him the glory! I still remember the time God found me even though I didn't want to be found. One Sunday in 2012 my auntie Vonnie Collier asked me to go with her to this church in downtown Memphis called "LOGIC" Light of Glory International Church. The pastor of LOGIC is a man by the name of Stephen Brown. Pastor Brown is in his mid-30s. Pastor Brown used to be my cousin Keith's basketball coach and that's how my auntie knew him. So, my aunt and I arrived at LOGIC for the first time one Sunday and as soon as I walked into the church I saw beautiful women everywhere. *I have to keep it real in this book.* During that period of time, I was still out gambling and running with the devil. I wasn't trying to hear what Pastor Brown was preaching about; I was too busy enjoying the scenery.

The next Sunday came around and I called my auntie and told her we needed to go to church. This time I kind of paid attention to Pastor Brown's teachings, but I was still looking at the beautiful women too. God knows how to pull a person in to get the word. I grasped enough of Pastor Brown's teaching that Sunday, and I actually went home and mediated on it. I was working at UPS at the time. My boss used to keep a bible on the table at our work station. After my second visited to LOGIC I promised myself that I would read at least five pages of the bible and one page of the devotional book every day at work.

Another Sunday came around and we went to LOGIC again. Pastor Brown opened up the doors of the church and he asked if anybody wanted to join the church. I made a decision that day that I wanted to accept Jesus Christ as my savior and join LOGIC. I also accepted Pastor Brown to become my spiritual leader to help me get on track with God. It felt so good joining the church that day. My auntie and a couple of my cousins joined the church that day too. In spite of everything I did in the past, God still saw the good in me. I can't explain the feeling that I got from giving my life to Christ!

Chapter 16 – Breaking the Family Curses

The devil has had several curses on my family for generations, and I'm sick of it. I took a stand to fight back against the enemy. God has really showed me favor and grace these past couple of years. God has giving me the strength and power to break some of my family generational curses. God has given me the wisdom and knowledge to conquer some of my personal adversaries that I have been dealing with as well. The last few years of my life have been very stressful and rewarding at the same time. I have achieved and accomplished things that I never would've dreamed of. I have been placed in positions that I wasn't qualified for. God has turned my life completely around, and I will forever give him the Glory. I never thought in a million years that I would be one of the persons in my family who gives the devil a run for his money. The crazy thing about it is God can do the same thing for you, if you let him. One thing I can say is the journey hasn't been easy, and I wanted to give up plenty of times. Every time I wanted to give up I thought to myself *this isn't about me*. The calling on my life is worth fighting for. Never forget that the calling on your life is worth fighting for. The fight is for my family! I have put on my boxing gloves, and I'm ready to rumble the devil!

Chapter 17 – Education Soars

Education is probably one of the curses I want my family to break the most. I understand that getting an education is supposed to be one of the most important things a person should strive to get. Unfortunately, getting an education wasn't my main priority when I was in high school. Even though I skipped the 11th grade and graduated from high school a year early, I didn't care about making good grades. I was more focused on trying to follow the crowd, and that wasn't a good thing to do. I graduated from Bolton High School with a 2.5 GPA weighed on a 4.0 scale. A 2.5 GPA is a 62 grade point average, which is a D. After I graduated from high school, I enrolled at Southwest Tennessee Community College. I still wasn't concerned about my education because getting a college degree wasn't normal where I'm from. I knew nobody who received a college degree. Everybody whom I knew dropped out of school in middle or high school. The ones who did graduate from high school either enrolled in college to receive a refund check or graduated from high school just to get a job at a warehouse.

I started community college in August of 2011. During my first year at Southwest Tennessee Community College I received average grades and I still was involved in the streets. I would make good grades in class but I wasn't retaining any of the information. I was just trying to pass. I didn't get serious about my education until my second year at Southwest. I took a good look at everything and everybody around me. I said to myself *I have to make a change.* I couldn't let my family members who were younger than me grow up thinking that education is not important, so I got serious with my education.

Getting an education was probably one of my main focuses starting off my second year at Southwest. I knew that I had to become a model for my entire family and friends. God told me that I will be the model for teenagers to get an education. God also told me even people older than I will go back to get an education because of me. I took everything that God told me and ran with it. I knew that I had to break the education curse that was over my family. I knew that it wasn't going to be easy but I knew if I had God with me that anything is possible. Nothing is too big for God.

I ended up graduating from Southwest Tennessee Community College with an Associate Degree in criminal justice. I graduated from Southwest with a 3.34 GPA in May of 2014. Graduating from college was a big accomplishment for me, because I was the first person in my family who graduated from college. I heard the chains falling from my family as I walked across the stage. My God! My God! That was a wonderful feeling getting a degree in criminal justice. I had broken one of my family's educational curses. I received a college degree, but I knew the job wasn't finished.

As soon as I graduated from Southwest Tennessee Community College I transferred to the University of Memphis. Getting an acceptance letter from the University of Memphis felt so unreal. The University of Memphis is one of the best colleges in Tennessee, but the acceptance letters didn't stop there. The next college that I received an acceptance letter from was the illustrious Clark Atlanta University. Clark Atlanta University is a historical black college. Receiving my acceptance from CAU was a huge accomplishment for me. My last acceptance letter came from the University of Chattanooga. UTC is a very good school to attend.

The university that I chose to attend and stay at was the University of Memphis, and I broke another curse by enrolling at a university. Nobody in my family ever enrolled in a four year university before. I think me taking the initiative to enroll in college opened up the minds of my family to do the same thing. My big cousin Vernon Pittman went to GED school and completed it. After he received his GED, he enrolled in college and graduated. I felt so good for my cousin because he helped me continue to break the family educational curse, but the graduations didn't stop with him. My little cousin Latisha graduated from high school. After that, she enrolled at a trade school and graduated. That was a major accomplishment for the family. Three people in the family graduated from college.

I'm glad that God granted me the strength to get an education so that I could push my family members to do the same thing. I'm currently pursing my Bachelor's degree at the University of Memphis. I have a 3.34 GPA. I'm a member of the NAACP chapter at the University of Memphis, and I'm a member of Alpha Phi Sigma National Criminal Justice Honors Society. I am also in the Criminal Justice Club. My God! My family will become doctors, lawyers, and other types of professions. The education curse is being broken! We all will be educated!

Chapter 18 –
Out of the Thug Life

I will never forget the time I made the decision to stop gangbanging and hanging around the wrong crowd. It was the year 2012 and my church was having a revival with a prophet. I will never forget what happened during one of the revival nights. My two best friends, Reginald and Tyrone came to church with me. As we were sitting down, the prophet was on the pulpit preaching. All of a sudden he said, "if your last name is Collier, stand up. There were only three people in my family at the revival at that time including me. So we stood up and he asked me for my name. I told him my name is Deangelo, and he replied, "Okay and he told my two cousins to sit down." The prophet said that God told him to tell me that if I don't stop hanging around the wrong crowd that I was going to end up dead. He also said that if I do stop hanging around the wrong crowd I was going to graduate from college and become successful. I was shocked when the prophet told me I was going to die if I don't stop hanging around the wrong crowd. It spooked me because I already was thinking that something bad was going to happen to me because I was hanging around the wrong crowd. I had gotten so scared that I was kind of skeptical about going to MTSU the next weekend. The prophet gave me a confirmation and I took heed to it. I knew I had to let the street life go.

Losing my loved ones to the streets contributed to me changing my life around. I knew I couldn't continue the curse because my younger family members were in jeopardy of going down the wrong road. Getting out of my comfort zone and trusting God was probably the hardest, but smartest thing I ever had to do! No more robbers! No more gang members in my family. No more drug dealers in my family! The street life curse is being broken!

Chapter 19 – Spiritual Life

God is the head of my family, but he hasn't always been. My family always believed in God but when everybody moved from Gallaway to Memphis we stopped going to church. We didn't have a church home and my grandmother's church was too far away. My grandmother was the spiritual leader in our family until she was forced to move to Memphis from Gallaway because of illness. My grandma is a dedicated Holy Ghost filled lady, but her sudden illness stopped her from going to church.

None of my family including me went to church on a regular basis until the year 2012. My family and I came to our senses and realized that God has been too good to us for us to not worship him. We knew that we had to rededicate our life to Christ. My auntie Vonnie, ten of my cousins, and I joined Light of Glory International Church with Pastor Stephen Brown. My sister Ebony and my two nieces, Natalya and Jernya, joined my sister's father's church. My auntie Pamela joined another church. I'm so happy that my family and I rededicated our life to Christ. I got a feeling that my whole family will get out of the streets and dedicate their lives to Christ. We will serve the Lord! The spiritual curse will be broken! My family belongs to God! My whole family is going to be saved!

Chapter 20 – Government Ties

It seems as if my family has been getting into trouble with the law for as long as I can remember. Mostly every dude in my family over age 18 has been to jail before. The getting in trouble with the law curse in my family had been haunting my family for a long time, and I knew I had to break the cycle. One day while enrolled at the University of Memphis my academic advisor emailed me about an internship opportunity. The internship was for the Shelby County District Attorney General's Office. I thought to myself *this can be a good networking opportunity*. I filled out the internship application and sent it to the SCDAG office. A few days later I received an email about an interview for the internship. To make a long story short, I started my internship for the SCDAG office in September of 2014. I was so happy that God made that possible for me. The internship consisted of being a truancy officer for the Shelby County District Attorney General's Office. I was so happy with my internship. It was a great experience, but all of a sudden something happened. I never knew in a million years that my life could make such a change.

One day in June of 2015, my boss at the SCDAG called for a meeting. She was telling us that there was about to be a change with the interns and employees. She asked me and one of the young ladies who was interning with me if we wanted to become official employees at the SCDAG office. I couldn't do anything but say yes and look up to God to tell him thank you. How many people actually go from an intern to an employee while still enrolled in college? I'm so thankful that my boss offered me the position. I thank God for my boss. With that position, I broke my family generational getting in trouble with the law curse. I'm somewhat the first person in my family to actually work for the government in the criminal justice system. My mom worked for a federal prison about fifteen years ago. I know that my family will stop getting in trouble with the law. This curse is being broken!

Chapter 21 – Giving Back

Everybody in my family has a good loving and kind heart, but we really never did any kind of community outreach. My family is not stingy with money or anything like that. I guess one of the reasons why my family never did any outreach or donated anything to another family was because of laziness, but that's about to stop. In 2015, God put it on my heart to do a lot of outreach and giving back. My heart melts when I see a family hurting because of financial problems. I hate seeing people living in poverty. I'm not rich but I always try to help people in need. I don't care if I have $100 in my pocket; if I see a person hungry I will instantly buy that person something to eat. I do it because of the God in me. God said we should never let our neighbor go hungry if we have the power to prevent it.

I started giving back last year in August. In August of 2015, I donated 25 backpacks full of school supplies to my hometown Gallaway, Tennessee. I thank God for giving me the mind to want to help my hometown. The 25 backpacks with the school supplies cost around three hundred dollars. I had around five hundred dollars in the bank at the time, but I still donated because I felt that the kids in my hometown needed school supplies for school. They needed the school supplies so they can get an education to break their family curses.

I thank my two friends, Eric and Shedrick, for helping me pull off that awesome outreach event. They gave me half of the money to purchase the school supplies. I'm very big on outreach and helping the community because the community needs it. Also, my friend Eric and I gave away three Thanksgiving baskets to three families in need. I gave away Thanksgiving baskets to two families in my hometown Gallaway. Eric gave away his turkey basket to one of his Facebook friends.

There are people in my hometown and all across the world who are starving, and without a place to stay, especially the homeless. I hope God puts it in my family's spirit and me to give back to the less fortunate. In the future, I pray that my family, the rest of the world, and I will put it in our hearts to go out and make a difference in somebody else's life.

Chapter 22 - No Drugs

Drugs have been one of the mild curses in my family, but still noticeable. Most of my male cousins do drugs. They either smoke marijuana or take pills illegally. I must admit that I smoked weed one time. I was fifteen years old and I was on a family trip with one of my friends. I did it because I was trying to be cool, but I haven't smoked weed ever since then. I knew I couldn't carry on this generational curse. I had to become a positive model for my family. I don't do drugs, and the family members who are younger than me will not do drugs. The people in my family who are doing drugs will stop doing drugs in the future.

Doing drugs is pointless. I understand that people do drugs to relieve their stress but once the drugs wear off the stress comes back. No longer will the devil have a drug addiction curse on my family. I took the initiative to let the drug addiction stop with me. I couldn't continue to keep the family tradition going. I don't care if people think I'm lame for not doing drugs. The battle I'm facing is not about me. It is about my family, and I will continue to be lame if it's for my family's sake.

Chapter 23 - No Gambling

Gambling has been an ongoing curse in my family. Mostly everybody in family has done some type of gambling in their life. I have a few people in my family who still go to the casino. I personally had a gambling addiction and it was so hard to break. I used to shoot dice every day all day, but one day I came to the conclusion that I couldn't continue to be a product of the devil. I knew that I had to stop gambling for the sake of my family. I didn't want my nieces or little cousins to become gambling addicts when they got older.

I made a promise to God in 2013 that I would never shoot dice again any day of my life. I went cold turkey, and I thank God for giving me the strength to overcome my shooting dice addiction. I knew that gambling wasn't the only way to get money. I had to put it in my mind that shooting dice wasn't my source of getting money. My source is God. I have faith that the few relatives in my family who still shoot dice will stop in the near future. I have faith that they will make God their source of getting money. I have no worries because the gambling curse will continue to be broken!

Chapter 24 - Speaking Engagement

I have never been the type of person to speak out in public or anything of that sort. Nobody wanted to put a microphone in my hand because all I knew was negativity. The only thing I could've talked about at a speaking engagement was fighting, gambling, and hanging around the wrong crowd. Speaking engagements are designed to lift up, motivate, and inspire people. I couldn't even picture myself during my teenage years speaking to a large crowd, better yet motivating them, but out of nowhere all of that changed.

Once God gave me the wisdom and knowledge to change my thinking I started getting offers to speak at events. Every time someone asked me to come speak at an event, I went. I remember this one time in 2015 one of my coworkers, Chanel asked me if I could speak and give some knowledge to the youth at the Boys & Girls Club. I told her yes, and it felt so good sharing wisdom with them. All I could do was look up at the sky and thank God for turning my life around. I also had to thank Chanel for offering me that opportunity. She could've chosen anybody but she chose me, and I'm forever grateful for that.

I have a powerful testimony, and I am humble enough to use my testimony to change lives. If my words can prevent somebody from going down the wrong path, I'm all for it. I love speaking to the youth and people my age because I want every last one of them to become successful. I don't want the youth to become victims of the street life. I don't want the youth to be in gangs. I don't want them to go to jail. For the ones who are in gangs and involved in the street life, I pray that my testimony has changed their thinking. I love speaking engagements. My testimony has power, and I'm going to use it to change lives. I am going to give the devil a run for his money!

Chapter 25 – Testimony Still Loading

Although God has helped me overcome a lot of trials and tribulations in my life, I still have a long way to go. My full testimony is nowhere near complete. I'm facing new trials and tribulations every day, but I know if I don't give up this too shall come to pass. My daily walk with God is a struggle. Temptation is everywhere, but I know the calling that is on my life is worth fighting for. I'm nowhere near perfect, and I mess up every day. I'm not where I want to be in life, but I thank God that I'm not where I used to be. Maybe once I overcome some of the trials and tribulations in my life right now I will write another book. Until then, keep the faith, and keep fighting the good fight because WE ARE ALL GOING TO MAKE IT!!!

About the Author

I am twenty two years old. I was born in a place about thirty minutes outside of Memphis called Gallaway, Tennessee. I was raised in a single-parent household by my mother. I used to be a gang member until God turned my life around. I've obtained an Associate degree in Criminal Justice, and I'm currently pursing my BA degree at the University of Memphis. I have a passion for helping the youth reach their full potentials.

www.ingramcontent.com/pod-product-compliance
Lightning Source LLC
LaVergne TN
LVHW041549070426
835507LV00011B/1012